A Special Gift From God

TERRI L. REAVES

ILLUSTRATED BY: TERESA A. HARWELL

I would like to dedicate this book
to two very special people in my life
which would be Charles and Makiyo Burris.
They are really special gifts from God.
Also to Charlie's Special Angels—
a fundraising organization for children with autism.

A very special thanks goes to Teresa A. Harwell,
who is the illustrator of "A Very Special Gift From God".
Thank you so much for all your help.
God bless each and every one of you who took the time out
to help me through my journey.
Although this is a new road for me, I am enjoying the trip.

Terri L. Reaves

Hello, my name is Lizzie, and this is my brother

Tommy—we're twins.

Before we were born, Mommy and Daddy said

they were expecting 2 girl babies. So Tommy

was a big surprise because he was born as a boy.

Mommy named him after Daddy: "Thomas". We

call him Tommy!

Mommy said that we were two of the best things

that ever happened to her and my Daddy. She

said we were gifts from God.

And my brother Tommy, he was a special gift

because he has autism. Autism is where there is a

problem within his brain like "sensory problems".

To look at Tommy, you would never know he was different. Tommy doesn't talk much but he loves music, TV, and especially hot wheel cars. He can name almost any car he can see. Daddy says he has a special gift of knowing cars like that, which is a gift that a lot of autistic people have. It can be numbers, music, or even cars and trucks.

Tommy loves to wrestle with my Dad all the time

too. We all try to spend time with Tommy.

Sometimes when we go out, Tommy gets really

scared and screams really loud. Mommy says the

world through Tommy's eyes is way too big and

scary. He tries to block out noises by covering

his ears and closing his eyes, and even rocking.

Usually, Mommy or Daddy takes him away until

he calms down.

Mommy says God only gives children like Tommy

to special people—people with a lot of love to

give, and we should consider ourselves especially

blessed for our special gift from God, Tommy!

What is Autism?

Autism is when our brains are wired differently from others. Our social and communications skills are not the same as a normal person. Having autism doesn't mean we are not smart individuals; it just means we think quite different. There are different spectrums with having autism. Some spectrums are from having childhood disintegrative disorder, pervasive developmental disorder-not otherwise specified (PDD-NOS) and Asperger's Syndrome (ASD). The knowledge of a child being diagnosed with autism is now more prevalent. Early diagnoses are the best diagnoses. For example, failure to diagnose a child at an early age versus when he/she turns five causes this child to miss out on valuable opportunities for development.